All through the Storm

A walk with words

Original Photographs and Poems by
Sidney Crawford

AuthorHouse™
1663 Liberty Drive
Bloomington, IN 47403
www.authorhouse.com
Phone: 833-262-8899

Because of the dynamic nature of the Internet, any web addresses or links contained in this book may have changed
since publication and may no longer be valid. The views expressed in this work are solely those of the author and do not
necessarily reflect the views of the publisher, and the publisher hereby disclaims any responsibility for them.

Any people depicted in stock imagery provided by Getty Images are models,
and such images are being used for illustrative purposes only.
Certain stock imagery © Getty Images.

This book is printed on acid-free paper.

ISBN: 978-1-6655-5949-2 (sc)
ISBN: 978-1-6655-5950-8 (e)

Print information available on the last page.

Published by AuthorHouse 05/26/2022

authorHOUSE®

All through the Storm is dedicated first to my family. Without their love and support, none of this would be possible and I can't thank them enough. Secondly, to my friends, specifically Megan Trupp and Shauna Martin. You were always there to encourage and help me through this process. Love you guys, I genuinely could not have completed this without you and I'm so grateful to have friends like you in my life.

TO MY READERS...

Ever since I was a little girl, I always found that my thoughts came out best on paper. The things that I could see and feel but couldn't quite say, would all of a sudden come out clearly when I wrote them down. Poetry gave me the freedom to express my feelings without needing to speak.

All through the Storm is a collection of poems that I wrote while growing up. It is divided into three sections that represent different phases of healing. *All through the Storm* begins in the midst of a storm, where your feelings are beyond what you can understand; hard to feel and hard to read. As the clouds start to break, the next section shows you the first glimpse of hope. All of a sudden, your questions start to have some answers and with the lessons come the trust that hope is there. Finally, the sky begins to clear and you begin to see who you are underneath the debris left behind. The final section becomes your statement of identity, who you want the world to see and who you want the world to remember. These poems were not written in the order they appear, as real life doesn't flow through three phases so nicely. However, I have always found in my life that eventually the hard times lead to lessons, and those lessons lead to you discovering who you are.

Accompanying many of the poems are various photographs that I took during simple walks and hikes over the years. These walks, and as a result the pictures, were reminders to me of the beauty that exists in the world without having to be anything. Many themes in the poems were inspired by things I saw, particularly in the weather and in nature. I always found that the beauty of the words was best accompanied by the beauty of the world.

I hope you enjoy reading about the lessons I've learned from life and to anyone who has struggled with similar feelings, keep going. Eventually, the sky does clear, and it's worth waiting to see.

Happy Reading

- Sidney Crawford

It has been said a picture is worth 1000 words
So, pictures and words are worth
more than you've ever heard
Let your pictures be a banner and your words an anthem
For no matter what you believe, the world
will never be the same without them

IN THE STORM

A TIME OF GRIEVING...

THE UNEXPLAINABLE FEELINGS

A Letter for what I can't tell you

Today, there is a fog in my mind
And a thick cloud in my throat
There are bricks in my feet
And a dampness to my coat

Today, I limp through life
And stagger through my words
I choke on my fears
And my eyes? Hazy and blurred

There is a sad tune I cannot turn down
And a million ants crawling all around
I feel a volcano rumbling deep in my chest
And a jackhammer starts when I try to rest

There are frogs in every place that I step
And the bees in my head cause quite a fret
My umbrella is permanently stuck upside down
And someone just asked me why do I frown?

I know, right now, I cannot speak.
So, you may never understand
But it's kind of you to stay here
Even when I won't hold your hand

This is what it feels like,
For me when I stop.
I'll be alright
But at the same time right now I'm not

Please don't leave
I'm still here
And when the storm passes
I'll make sure to let you back near

I just wanted to let you know
What it's like and why I can't explain it
It's everything and nothing, but it hurts
I still love you please don't forget that

I am not afraid of the dark
I'm not afraid of being alone
I'm afraid of being here
Blind and with a heart of stone

The Days we Live For

Maybe the best dreams happen when you're awake
But honestly, right now, I'd rather be asleep
It's 1:48 am and nothing's entirely wrong
But it's certainly not right
Some days are bad before they begin,
But then I remember them as the best days
It's not entirely wrong, though I don't think it's right
Maybe I'm destined to live for the bad days
I do take comfort in them, they're familiar
The good days scare me, they don't seem real, so the good days are spent waiting for the bad
It doesn't make the good less good, nor the bad less bad
Sometimes, I don't even know the difference
Some days just are.
Most days just are,
It's not entirely wrong, just not right

The memories replay
I let them go but they stay
I can't escape what I was made to feel
Most days, I'm not even sure what's real

Same Different

Please, don't be afraid
They push me and pull me
But endlessly repeat that phrase,
Will I ever be free?

I could walk out the door
Step into the hall and find other's there
But I actually can't, not anymore
I can merely stay and whisper a prayer

There is not a lot of hope left
And what can be found isn't strong
My happiness is gone, I blame theft
Maybe we're just doomed to sing the wrong song

But then you remember others have bad days
So, you diminish again because maybe we're all the same
But you misunderstand, the beauty is not all our similar ways
It's the ways we're all different yet loved just the same

Are you sad today, my dear?
Please don't be afraid to shed some tears
Take your time and rest tonight
But tomorrow, get up and make things right

When Darkness Thrives

When darkness thrives,
How do you survive,
When it hurts to be alive
And there's nothing left for which to strive?

Do you sit back and wait?
Watching life go by day after day
Hoping to wake up to everything changed
To suddenly see there is another way

Do you grab life by the shirt,
and throw him to the dirt?
Stomp in his face, getting mud on your skirt
Finding yourself alone and still full of hurt

Do you run and run, until you reach the end?
Never looking back or trying to mend
Run till your problems are the only ones you tend
Finally stopping, and seeing no one around to call a friend

When darkness shows
Please God, tell me where do you go?
Because I'll tell you flat, I just don't know
And the darkness often just seems to grow

But don't worry, for I am still here
Amongst all the scars and all of my tears
Living despite being surrounded by fears
And knowing deep in my heart, You are still near

So, I will sit and wait for a while
Then grab life by the shirt and fight for a mile
And run and run until I find my true style
And through it all, I'll find some way to smile

My reason is I believe in you
I believe there must be something you've called me to do
And so, even if every day I have to start new
I'll find some way to return to you

When the going gets tough,
And the tough fall to their knees
It's the wise who bow their heads,
Say a prayer and whisper, please

One More Prayer

Am I wrong when I believe we all have a voice,
One that is meant to speak and make its own choice?
Am I wrong when I say there is more I can do,
Even if they say I don't necessarily need to?
Am I wrong to fight for a chance to be different,
To write my own story, to lead and feel, with no indifference?
Am I wrong to be scared of standing still,
Bending and breaking to please another's will?
Am I wrong to say I don't care what others think of me?
Because there is only One, who's vision truly sees
Maybe I'm wrong to dream and fight,
Maybe I'm too young and naïve to show the light,
Maybe I'm going off the rails and losing respect from all those
around me, maybe I'll wake up one day and realize just how
wrong I was.
But
What if I'm not wrong?
What if there is a special role for me,
What if I can be all I dream?
What if I can make a difference in the lives of those around me
and change our lives together,
For the better.
What if all it takes is one more prayer?

Look in the mirror, do you recognize who you see?
Even when our reflection isn't who we thought they'd be
God holds us tight and waits for you and me
And one day, we'll look and finally see,
That girl in the reflection is an absolute beauty

I don't like staying up late

I don't like staying up late
But some nights my eyes won't shut
And my brain lets all its thoughts out the gate
It is here, I see my life from outside the rut

You see, during the day I have the light
And I cling to the hope it offers for finding things
But there are certain things only found at night
When no voices call, no sun shines and no bird sings

I don't like staying up late
But the words come out different when I do
It's no longer a want, but a fate
To dictate things I didn't know to be true

Do you still believe good comes from the light?
Am I still sure I can even tell what is good?
For I look out my window and see the stars bright
And in this moment, all is as it should

I remember now, I used to like staying up late
The dark was fun and friends were many
We could laugh and share with endless stories to relate
As for the worry of being tired? Simply wasn't worth a penny

I think as the years went by
I bought into a story that said our lives should be light
And forgot that the world was not made on this lie
But on the promise of both a day and a night

So, today I think I will stay up late
And look at the stars and the city lights
And I'll look at the dark parts of me, the ones I wished not to create
And give them the love they have needed all through this life

And for once, maybe I will sleep
Knowing I don't have to fight, I never had to fight
For the worst parts of me have always been worthy to keep
And the truth: I would never have seen that amidst the light

THE BREAKING OF
THE CLOUDS

A TIME OF LEARNING...

DIFFICULT QUESTIONS AND THE EMERGENCE OF HOPEFUL ANSWERS

What do I do?

Why is it so easy to fear?
When all the world draws you near
And their words scream but all you hear
Is the drop on the table from a lonely tear

Why is it so easy to hide?
When people crowd everywhere but your side
And the expectations rise like the lunar tide
But the waves only come from all you've cried

When you've been held to the ground
And the cuts bleed but can't be found
You've gone left and right to turn your life around
And opened your mouth yet made no sound

Are you wondering if you failed?
If you drove your train right off the rails
And the ones you fought will no doubt prevail
It is at this moment, don't you let that fire go stale

If we believe in something enough for which to fight,
If we know without other's opinions that we are right
Then, maybe, it's your turn to invent the light
And remember 10 000 times Thomas Edison saw nothing but night

You've got another shot to fight to care
To use what you know and fill the air
And you may doubt, and they'll say it's not fair
But all you'll ever need is one more prayer

So, go be a beast you beautiful girl
Speak with truth and share with the world
Don't be afraid when the heads start to turn
And never let us forget while we're here we might as well learn

Your life won't be written in one day or even two
In fact, sometimes the best ending can only come for you
When you lay the poem down and put yourself to sleep
And in the morning with a pen in hand,
remember all you dreamed to keep

The Secret of Life

Leaves fall
Nature calls
I see it all
Yet still I stall

Waiting
Just waiting
Is something coming,
Or just fading?

I'm listening
And learning
But a laugh
May be all I'm yearning

I think connections
Are just protection
From seeing yourself
Needing correction

Or maybe being alone
Is a fear of being your own
And we need another
To take us home

Still watching
Just trudging
Not too slow, nor too fast
No, time's not budging

No leaves now
See straight to the sky
And wonder how many feathers
It might take to fly

Or whether one day
We'll understand our lives
Aren't far away
But look down by your side

See? You're not
Where you began
Which means you walked
If not, ran

So, waiting got you
Where you had to go
And the only place you had to go
Is exactly where I find you

It's not about where,
It's not about when
not about who
But is, and am, and are and true

Never let the tide move you from your walk
For when the waves crash, that's
when the world needs a rock

The Voice of Life

Sunshine keeps me watching
But no matter the fear of night
Why must the sun shine brightest
Just before it loses it's light?

Rain keeps me dancing
When the world falls around me
Why do the clouds join in,
When my only solution is to pretend to not see?

Storms keep me silent
As they crash against my heart
Why must we wait for the pounding to cease,
Just to restart?

Wind keeps me moving
For when I stand too long
Loneliness becomes beautiful
And solo becomes my favourite song

I suppose without the weather
I might forget the safety of being together
I might forget that a rest is necessary to train
And the best moments involve dancing to avoid the rain

And the sun disappears for a while
But it always comes back
So, I'll sit by my window and smile
Knowing there's nothing I truly lack

Thank you for this day
This life and this world
Thank you for the lessons you say
When the weather speaks to this girl

I pray we'll always listen
And live our lives to learn
Beauty will always glisten
And love will always return

Rise and shine, the most glorious phrase
That I truly hope guides your way
For if all you do is to rise and to shine
It will be a most wonderful day

Just Before Winter

I am a tree just before winter
Branches bare, leaves dead on the ground
No colours left
Surrounded by a silence of the heaviest sound

I am a tree just before winter
And the wind whistles through my aching limbs
The world stares and wishes for another season
For even snow would add a sparkle to the grim

I am a tree just before winter
No birds left landing on my branches
or butterflies to flutter in my sight
Nothing grows, but there's nothing left to die
Too late for leaves, and too early for lights

Waiting, waiting, waiting
I am a tree just before winter
But even winter is better than this
For gray and still, I wouldn't even take a picture

As I watch the end of one season and await the start of another
I feel a tear fall, but this one is not my own
I look and a child sits beneath
I wait, but her head only stays low

I am a tree just before winter
I creak and it breaks the silence
I'm the twig who can't bare the cold anymore
And snaps in utter defiance

The girl looks up after the fallen twig
And smiles as she sees the sunlight falling on her face
A squirrel scurries up my branch
And she takes a picture right there in that place

You see, I am a tree just before winter
Who has lost its leaves and is now ready for the snow to fall
Who's endured the transformation
And at their absolute worst still stood tall

And though I wait and know not what comes next
I am still around and soon the seasons will change
If nothing else, I offer the advice to look up
And see that the way we impact others is often strange

I am a tree just before winter
Who knows now its okay to rest
For whether mid-season, off-season or between
It is our existence that makes us our best

There's beauty in the sun and the cold in the dark
There's beauty in the faint of cries and the pure of hearts
There's beauty in silence and even in the screams
There's beauty anywhere you can find a few dreams

The World Cries

The rain falls on the roof outside my window
The world is crying today, I'm not sure why,
Is everything wrong?
No, maybe everything is just right

Maybe today, the world knows that life gets hard
That blisters and bruises, broken bones and hearts
Are not indications of error in our life,
But of chances we took and the depths of our fights.

Maybe today, someone told her, her dream would never come true,
But her strength and bravery pointed to a different view.
She saw those who came before her, who did what they couldn't
And finally believed that it could too.

Maybe today, she recognizes we are all angry some days
And she's taken the chance to yell and break a few plates
And standing in the middle of her shattered mess,
She finally makes the choice to forgive herself.

Maybe the world cries because for once everything is right
Not because it never went wrong, but because it never stayed that way
And today she's ready to try again
And take a chance on what she has to say

So, the world cries and I can't say I know what to do with her
But I will no longer sit by my window and watch her
Today, I take a step out the door and live in her rain
And yes, I am soaked with her joy and her pain

But as the rain falls, I feel just a little bit lighter
For with every tear she cries, the world appears a little brighter
I am crying today, I'm not sure why
I thought everything was wrong,
Turns out, it may be just right

When the night calls you to not let it end
Sit with yourself, take a moment, and listen
For the world has always been your friend
And you never want to miss a chance to see it glisten

The Clearing
of the Sky

A time of discovery...

Strength in knowing who you are and where you stand

I Choose Death

What are the moments we live for?
I can think of a few
Are they worth more than the moments we die for?
I guess that's up to you

The moments when all is wrong
But inside, you are right
The moments when the storm crashes
But your boat sails on to the light

The moments when you laugh
And someone else smiles
When you try something you've never done
When you think, man, I haven't done this in a while

When you realize you're worthy of love
And take a chance to reach out
When someone thinks of you when you feel small
And gives a kind word when all you've heard are shouts

These are some of the moments we live for
Love, laughter, peace and hope
Beautiful no doubt, but the truth of life
Some moments leave us nothing, no choice but to cope

The moments when you bare your teeth
Though surrounded by wolves
And when you throw that punch
In a ring that never offered you gloves

When you find one alone
And you stand up and take their place
When you change the story you have been told
And do it right in a hater's face

When you take a chance on your own idea
And give your all to show others
That what you've discovered is how its supposed to be
When you wait because all you need is one other

Fight, grit, perseverance, and patience
These are the moments you die for
Sometimes you ignore these things
Because who really wants to die more?

But the unfortunate fact in this thing called life
Is that each one of us will live, and each will die
And in most cases throughout history
You won't know why

So, if you must do both
Why not do each well?
If we are going to live for something
Why not die with something to tell?

Why not give your life fighting for us,
For you, for them, for the world
For the people, for the families
For each boy and each girl

Anyone can live everyday
You don't even have to try to do that
But the special choice, is whether or not
you choose to die each day
Will you fight and face all that you can't?

Dying to the old self and the old ways
Dying to what you can't be and looking only for what you strive
You cannot truly live, unless you first learn to die
For it is only in our own death, we realize
that which truly keeps us alive

When time slows down, and the world stands still
When your path changes course, whether up or downhill
That's when we need to listen, take a moment look to heaven,
and say with one single promise
"I will"

Weather or not

I am the weather and
Rain, snow or shine will change
Me to believe in life.
Change is my way to live,
Nothing is right, at least
Not always, time and place
For everything and
Plans fail, but I can live
As long as I can change.
I can be whoever
And life will not hold me.
No, in fact, it cannot.
Life won't be able to
Keep up with my weather.
It will release me and
I will be free to change
Because no matter what,
I am doing something,
And doing is living
And to live, is the dream

When the world tells you it's time to stop the words
Remember the singing of all the little birds
Who never let those around them dictate their song
And speak the truth that you've known all along

My Rock

I stood on my rock awaiting the waves crashing down
They watched from the safety of their familiar ground
"She's crazy, leave her be."
But still they stared, praying for me
I smiled as they mocked and the waves grew higher
For deep in my heart, there grew such a fire
They screamed, "Please, come back to shore!"
But little do they know, my rock means so much more
The waves hit and I stood, soaked but not drowned
But they, were nowhere to be found
I looked to my feet and there it still remained
Unharmed, strong, and always the same
The rock we choose to stand on governs many things
But most importantly, after the storm hits, will you have a place to stand and sing?

The world spun and the words hit hard
My life it spiralled, I was all out of cards
I fell to the ground, but you see from
down there I could see it all
To see my final move, I just needed to fall

What it means to be Kind

In the end, I finally understand
What it takes to truly be kind
I must stand and oppose all that is not
Oh, how the world will be so disappointed in me

And together we stand
With our hearts in our hands
Unafraid because even in a world
that's tried to keep you down
We have hope, knowing your story will
be the one to come around

I am the Flower

I knew a flower once,
She grew up kind and bright
And the sun shone for her.
One day the rain started
And it rained and it rained.

I knew a flower once,
Who stood the rain for years,
Whose roots were soaked and drowned
Yet she stood and waited.

I knew a flower once,
Who got out of the rain
Only to watch a brick fall
And leave not one piece of
The poor flower untouched.

I knew a flower once,
I thought that she was dead
But I picked the brick up
Just to see what was left

I knew a flower once,
And found she was still there,
A few missing leaves and
She didn't stand so tall.
Now, the sun seemed to miss
Her and she didn't sway
with the wind but tilted.

I knew a flower once,
I looked at her real close,
And found she was still kind
And bright and alive and
The sun must hit her, if
Not all the time, enough.

I knew a flower once,
And she taught me that you
Don't leave life the same way
That you enter in it.
A little bit more bruised,
A little more fragile,
Not the pretty story.

I knew a flower once,
Who didn't know why life
Hit her the way it did
But I showed her these words.
The only flower I
Wrote about, was the one
Who was crushed by a brick.

So, I sat with flower
And we talked about life
And what she was going
To do now that she was
Alive again. Now that
The rain stopped and the brick
Picked up, leaving her free.

She looked around and said,
"This is my new chapter
The one I didn't write,
This is the one life wrote
For me, all I have to
Do now, is turn the page"

And tonight, I'll close my eyes and I will pray.
When ignoring the words becomes too much,
Instead, I thank God that I am just a girl
For it's always been more than enough

The End

The next year comes faster than we think
Do we stop, take it in and dwell with a drink?
Or run headfirst because we know we're on the brink
Of something amazing, even though the beginning is an end that makes our hearts sink

It's hard to let go when you've waited so long for what you have
But maybe there's something even greater in your plan
The truth is you've never before had something to leave behind
That's why for the first time your brain is begging you to rewind

But this is good, even though it doesn't feel like it should
You loved, you were loved and you are not forgotten
You helped, you laughed and did all you never knew you would
That's why you can stand proud of everything you've gotten

You earned a beautiful summer
And yes, the ending is quite a bummer
But the beauty of one good chapter
Is that maybe you have another one after

They don't tell you the problem with learning to live
Is that it hurts so much more when all that's left is the end to give
But your life still has worth and still matters
And love will find you and you won't be shattered

Have faith and patience, you will be alright
It's okay to be scared and stay up late one night
But soon, the day does end and a new one begins
And what's in store for you may be another big win

Take the step, make the leap, believe in you
You've got this far and you're so close
This world isn't going to know what hit 'em
But you, you're going to raise your glass for a toast

To all the lives you lived in your short time
To all the goodbyes that made you cry
To all the smiles and the highs
And to everything you've ever heard in your mind

Everything is your story
Good, bad, messy, glory
Time to let go and let love in
You're ready, the end is the time to begin

Printed in the United States
by Baker & Taylor Publisher Services